Weird
Wonders
of the
Deep
An Imagination Library Series

Anglerfish

by Valerie J. Weber

GARETH**STEVENS**
PUBLISHING
A WRC Media Company

Please visit our web site at: www.garethstevens.com
For a free color catalog describing Gareth Stevens Publishing's
list of high-quality books and multimedia programs,
call 1-800-542-2595 (USA) or 1-800-387-3178 (Canada).
Gareth Stevens Publishing's fax: (414) 332-3567.

Library of Congress Cataloging-in-Publication Data available upon request from publisher.
Fax (414) 336-0157 for the attention of the Publishing Records Department.

ISBN 0-8368-4560-9

First published in 2005 by
Gareth Stevens Publishing
A WRC Media Company
330 West Olive Street, Suite 100
Milwaukee, WI 53212 USA

Cover design and page layout: Scott M. Krall
Series editors: JoAnn Early Macken and Mark J. Sachner
Picture Researcher: Diane Laska-Swanke

Photo credits: Cover, pp. 5, 9, 11, 13, 17, 19 © E. Widder/HBOI/Visuals Unlimited;
p. 7 © Makoto kubo/e-photography/SeaPics.com; p. 15 © Rudie Kuiter/SeaPics.com;
p. 21 © Bob Cranston/SeaPics.com

Printed in the United States of America

1 2 3 4 5 6 7 8 9 09 08 07 06 05

Front cover: An anglerfish waits in the darkness.
The lure on this one grows just above its upper lip.
The lure lights up to attract other animals to eat.

Table of Contents

Words that appear in the glossary are printed in **boldface** type the first time they occur in the text.

One Gulp, Then Gone

Deep in the sea, a tiny light glows. It flashes on and off. A small fish gets curious — is this food? Too late, sharp teeth surround the tiny swimmer. In one gulp, the fish goes down the anglerfish's throat. The anglerfish's glowing **lure** has done its job.

Deep-sea anglerfish live in the darkest parts of the ocean, far from the light of the Sun. How do they find their **prey** — and each other? The anglerfish carries its own fishing pole growing right out of the top of its head. At the end of the pole dangles a lure that lights up. The lure draws in prey and might be used to attract a **mate**.

People often name anglerfish after the way they look. This one is called the warted sea devil. Its lure floats out in front of its mouth.

A Living Light

About 150 types of anglerfish swim deep in the ocean. Many other kinds live in shallower waters.

Deep-sea anglerfish differ from their cousins who live closer to the surface. The lures on those anglerfish do not light up.

The lures on deep-sea anglerfish contain a special kind of **bacteria**. The bacteria create the light. Each kind of anglerfish keeps a different kind of bacteria. No one knows exactly how the anglerfish gets its bacteria. The fish is not born with it, and the bacteria do not float around waiting to be caught.

This flat anglerfish lives in shallower waters than deep-sea anglerfish. For years, people have used anglerfish in Chinese medicine.

A Fin Like a Fishing Pole

In a world of darkness, any light draws the curious. Each kind of anglerfish carries its own different light **organ**. Some are shaped like the roots of a plant. Others look like tiny stalks or little whips.

The lure is attached to a fin on the front of the anglerfish. The fin acts like a fishing pole. On different kinds of anglerfish, the fin grows from different places. Some stand high on the fish's head. Others perch just above the upper lip. Some lie on the forehead between the eyes. Some are two or three times longer than the body of the fish. They trail out behind the fish as it swims.

This is a close-up of the lure on the bulbous dreamer anglerfish. It looks like a tiny fish. Other fish might think it will be a tasty snack. Wrong! Instead, they might become the anglerfish's meal.

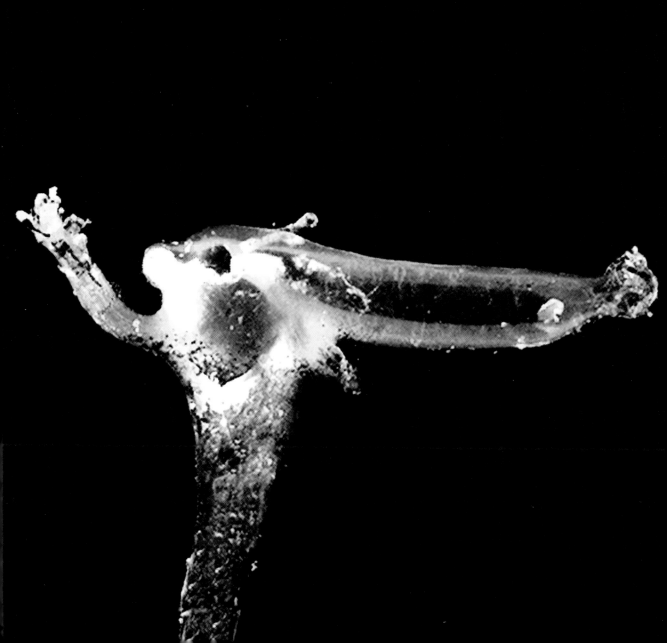

Hiding in the Dark

Anglerfish can control their lights, turning them on and off. This makes their prey more curious, drawing it in. The light may also be used to attract a mate.

Some anglerfish have more than lights on their heads. One anglerfish's scientific name says it all. In Greek, it means "toad that fishes with a net." The fish looks like a toad, and the net looks like seaweed fronds hanging from its jaw. The net lights up as well.

Even with its lures lit, the anglerfish stays in the dark. Its dark brown or black body **absorbs** the light from its lure. This helps it hide from possible prey and **predators**.

This bulbous dreamer's mouth gapes open. Even the inside of its stomach is black to absorb light. If the anglerfish eats a fish that lights up, a predator cannot see it inside the anglerfish.

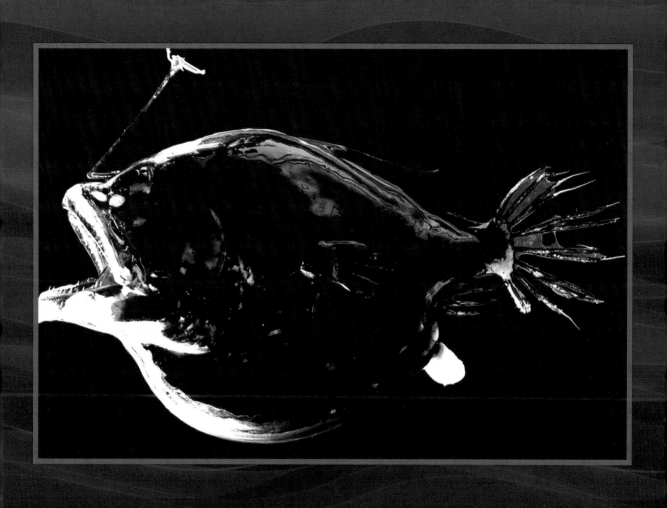

A Toothed Ball

Although their teeth are huge, most anglerfish are quite small. They look like tennis balls with teeth. Those needle-sharp teeth face backward. Most anglerfish grow to about 4 inches (10 centimeters). The largest reach more than 3 feet (1 meter) and can weigh almost 20 pounds (9 kilograms).

Anglerfish can swallow prey larger than themselves. Their jaws and stomachs stretch like rubber bands.

Unlike most other fish, anglerfish do not have regular scales. Instead, loose, thin skin — often with tiny spines — covers their bodies. When people try to grab an anglerfish from a deep-sea fishing net, the skin slides right off its body.

This blackdevil anglerfish can reach 5 inches (13 cm). Its back fin looks like a fan of feathers.

A Chilly, Dark Place

Anglerfish live down to at least 6,500 feet (2,000 m) below the surface. The water there is nearly freezing, about 39° Fahrenheit (2° Celsius).

The deep sea covers more than half the planet. No plants can grow down there because there is no sunlight. Bits of dead fish and plants float down from the surface. They provide one source of food for fish. Anglerfish also hunt other fish and **crustaceans**. Anglerfish even eat lantern fish, which often grow larger than the anglerfish!

Like anglerfish, brooch lantern fish also light up the dark ocean. Their light organs run along the lower part of their heads and bodies.

Two Different Fish?

Scientists once thought male and female anglerfish were two different kinds of fish! Males are one-tenth the size of females. They look like black jellybeans with fins. They are also more muscular than the fatter females. They have to be to swim long distances to find their mates.

Females are built to stay mostly in one place. **Ambush** hunters, they wait for prey to come to their lights.

An anglerfish known as the football fish can live down to at least 2,700 feet (830 m). The tiny males grow to only about 1 1/2 inches (4 cm).

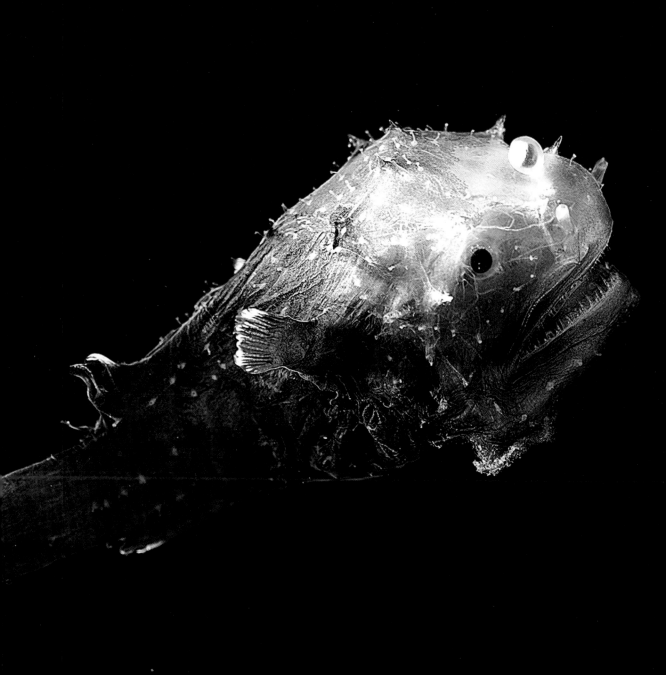

Big Mom, Little Dad

How does a fish live without eating? That's the question for some male deep-sea anglerfish. They have no lures to attract prey and no teeth to catch it.

What they do have are large eyes and a really good sense of smell. They can sniff out the scent the female anglerfish spread in the water. The males follow the smell.

When a male finds a female, special hooks on his snout and chin attach to her belly. In some kinds of anglerfish, the male's body slowly melts into the female's. Those large eyes disappear. All that is left of the male is his mouth to take in water. Her blood provides him with energy. A female anglerfish may have two or more males hanging from her.

A tiny male hangs from the belly of this female blackdevil anglerfish. He has tracked her through the dark ocean.

Going Down Deep

It was once impossible to look for anglerfish deep in the sea. Scientists only knew about them because they came up in deep-water fishing nets. People thought no life could exist far beneath the waves.

Now it is just very difficult. Scientists and **engineers** have developed **submersibles** that can explore underwater. Some submersibles carry drivers who **pilot** them. Others are controlled by people in a ship above. The unpiloted vehicles move like robots. They can take samples of deep-sea creatures, including the anglerfish.

With each trip to the deep, scientists find out more about anglerfish. Who knows what else will light up the dark seas?

The best pictures of anglerfish are taken from submersibles like this one. This two-person ship can go down to 3,000 feet (915 m). Its lights help show animals of the dark ocean as if they were in sunlight.

More to Read and View

Books (Nonfiction)   *Creeps from the Deep.* Leighton Taylor (Chronicle Books)
Deep Oceans. Living on the Edge (series). Wendy Pfeffer
(Marshall Cavendish)
Deep Sea Adventures: A Chapter Book. True Tale (series).
Kristen Hall (Scholastic Library Publishing)
Dive! A Book of Deep-Sea Creatures. Hello Reader! Science
(series). Melvin Berger (Scholastic)
The Great Undersea Search. Kate Needham (Usborne Publishing Ltd.)
Way Down Deep: Strange Ocean Creatures. Patricia Brennan Demuth
(Grosset & Dunlap)

Videos (Nonfiction)   *Blue Planet: Seas of Life: The Deep* (BBC Video)
Into the Abyss (Nova)

Places to Write and Visit

Here are three places to contact for more information:

**American Museum of
Natural History**
Central Park West
at 79th Street
New York, NY 10024
1-212-765-5100
www.amnh.org

The Florida Aquarium
701 Channelside Drive
Tampa, FL 33602
1-813-273-4000
www.flaquarium.net

**Maritime Aquarium at
Norwalk**
10 North Water Street
Norwalk, CT 06854
1-203-852-0700
www.maritimeaquarium.org

Web Sites

Web sites change frequently, but we believe the following web sites are going to last. You can also use good search engines, such as **Yahooligans!** [**www.yahooligans.com**] or **Google** [**www.google.com**], to find more information about anglerfish. Here are some keywords to help you: *anglerfish, deep-sea creatures, lanternfish, bulbous dreamer,* and *triplewart sea devil.*

ramseydoran.com/anglerfish/deep_sea.htm
Learn more about the anglerfish on this web site, complete with images.

www.amonline.net.au/fishes/students/focus/antdeep.htm
The Australian Museum online site contains brief information on anglerfish and great photos.

www.fishbase.org/ComNames/CommonNameSearchList.cfm
Look up various kinds of anglerfish and get detailed information on where they live and how big they get.

www.lifesci.ucsb.edu/~biolum/index.shtml
Find out how anglerfish and other animals light up the ocean.

www.mbayaq.org/efc/living%5Fspecies
The Monterey Bay Aquarium provides information on all kinds of fish, including anglerfish. Type in the name of the fish you are interested in and find out more.

Glossary

You can find these words on the pages listed. Reading a word in a sentence helps you understand it even better.

absorbs (ab–SORBS) — soaks up or takes in 10

ambush (AM-bush) — a surprise attack from a hidden place 16

bacteria (bak-TEER-ee-uh) — tiny, one-celled, living beings 6

crustaceans (krus-TAE-shuns) — animals with hard shells that live mostly in the water 14

engineers (en-juh-NEERS) — people who plan and build machines, bridges, or roads 20

lure (LOOR) — an object that strongly attracts an animal or person 4, 6, 8, 10, 18

mate (MATE) — a male or female of a pair of animals. Most kinds of animals need a mate to make babies. 4, 10, 16

organ (OR-gun) — a part of the body that does a particular job 8, 14

pilot (PI-lut) — to drive or steer 20

predators (PRED-uh-turz) — animals that hunt other animals for food 10, 14

prey (PRAY) — animals that are hunted by other animals for food 4, 10, 12, 16, 18

submersibles (sub-MUR-suh-buls) — ships that can go underwater 20

Index